AF725493

TTAIN-1717 : 2025

INTERNATIONAL STANDARD

SECOND EDITION

L'APPLICATION DE L'INTELLIGENCE ARTIFICIELLE DANS GESTION DE LA RELATION CLIENT PARTIE 1: EXIGENCES

THE APPLICATION OF ARTIFICIAL INTELLIGENCE IN CUSTOMER RELATIONSHIP MANAGEMENT PART 1: REQUIREMENTS

WWW.TOPTENAWARD.NET

Published by: Top Ten Award International Network Inc.
Vancouver, BC **CANADA**
Toll-Free No.: 1-778-751-8127
Email: Info@TOPTENAWARD.Net
www.TOPTENAWARD.Net

Ordering Information:
Quantity sales. Special discounts are available on quantity purchases by universities, schools, libraries, standard Institutes, regulatory organizations, corporations, associations, and others. For details, contact the "Sales Department" at the above mentioned email address.

The Application of AI in Customer relationship management, Part:1 Requirements/TTAIN—2nd Edition

ISBN 978-1-77899-035-9 Paperback

ISBN 978-1-77899-036-6 Hardcover

Punblished in North America (Canada, USA, Mexico) and Available in more than 40,000 bookstores.

Contents

About TTAIN

Top Ten Award International Network (TTAIN) is a premier skill development and official credentialing organization. TTAIN is an international organization dedicated to publishing educational books, developing standards, and offering educational services and certifications. Operating under industry-approved international standards, TTAIN ensures integrity and impartiality, prioritizing both professional and public interests.

TTAIN provides objective evidence that individuals and organizations meet the highest ethical, legal, professional, and technical standards. We certify a wide range of professionals and organizations, including government entities, businesses, and professional associations. Our International Award and certification programs are based on widely recognized national and international compliance standards, ensuring broad acceptance both domestically and globally.

International Credentials

TTAIN is a leading global body for skill development and certification, committed to excellence in compliance with International standards. These international standards form a unified system for evaluating and recognizing competent organizations worldwide. As a result, TTAIN is dedicated to maintaining high service standards and ensuring that we positively impact the businesses and professionals we serve.

Why We Decided to Help Professionals

Our journey toward helping professionals began after a pivotal experience: the shock of being fired. This forced us to acknowledge some hard truths:

Large companies often move too slowly, and many great ideas are lost in a sea of approvals.
Climbing the corporate ladder can hinder productivity, as we became more focused on promotions than on making meaningful progress.
Politics and office turf wars are inevitable in large organizations, leading to burnout and frustration. We wanted to focus on getting things done and improving our work, but instead, we were stuck in a constant struggle that negatively affected our health and happiness.
This realization inspired us to help others escape the same frustrations. Today, over 7100 professionals, employees, employers, teachers, and schools are actively using our International Standards, publications, educational materials, certifications, and training to bring their ideas, products, and services to the world.

Upgrading International Standards

At TTAIN, we are dedicated to upgrading the level of international standards by developing both applicational and operational standards that address real-world challenges. Our approach focuses on creating standards that are practical, measurable, and aligned with actual industry needs. This ensures that the standards we establish are not only theoretical but actionable, providing clear benchmarks for performance.

Our operational standards are designed to allow businesses and professionals to assess the effectiveness of their practices in real, measurable terms. We help organizations evaluate their outcomes through data-driven metrics and operational success, ensuring that the improvements made are tangible and not merely theoretical. By focusing on measurable effectiveness, TTAIN drives meaningful change and sets a new standard for global excellence.

It's time for you to unlock your blueprint for success.

Welcome to the Top Ten Award International Network (TTAIN).

Every effort has been made to ensure the accuracy of the information in this document at the time of publication. However, the publisher and author accept no responsibility for any errors or omissions, regardless of cause. They also disclaim liability for any loss or damage incurred by any person acting, or refraining from acting, based on the material in this publication.

THE APPLICATION OF ARTIFICIAL INTELLIGENCE IN CUSTOMER RELATIONSHIP MANAGEMENT
PART 1: REQUIREMENTS

AA Summary:

This standard aims to utilize artificial intelligence (AI) to enhance CRM systems and emphasizes the importance of adhering to ethical and technical standards in this field. AI can improve customer experience by analyzing big data, predicting needs, and optimizing responses. The use of AI must always be in compliance with ethical principles, privacy regulations, and applicable laws in different regions.

BB Scope:

This standard is for all organizations that use CRM systems to manage customer interactions and intend to utilize artificial intelligence (AI) technologies such as chatbots, machine learning, natural language processing (NLP), and other techniques in their processes. The standard covers all technical, ethical, and legal aspects of using AI in customer interactions with organizations.

CC Definitions:

CC-1- Artificial Intelligence (AI): Software systems capable of performing cognitive tasks similar to those of humans.
CC-2- CRM (Customer Relationship Management): Software systems that manage an organization's interactions with customers.
CC-3- Chatbot: Software capable of interacting with and responding to customer requests automatically.
CC-4- Machine Learning: A branch of AI that enables systems to learn from data and improve over time.
CC-5- Natural Language Processing (NLP): Technology that allows systems to analyze and understand human language.
CC-6- Personal Data: Information that can identify an individual, such as name, email address, phone number, and other sensitive information.

DD General Requirements:

DD-1-**Transparency:** Every AI algorithm used must be transparent, and users and customers should be informed that they are interacting with automated systems. For example, when using chatbots, these bots must inform customers that they are dealing with an automated system.

DD-2- **Accuracy and Precision:** AI models must have at least 95% accuracy in predicting and simulating customer interactions. If the model's accuracy is below this threshold, the model shall be retrained.

DD-3- **Privacy and Data Protection:** All personal and sensitive customer data shall be collected, stored, and processed according to the relevant laws and regulations in each region.

These laws should include the following:

European Union Laws (GDPR): Personal data must be collected, processed, and stored in accordance with the General Data Protection Regulation (GDPR) in the European Union.
United States Laws (CCPA): In compliance with the California Consumer Privacy Act (CCPA), customers must have the right to access, modify, and delete their personal data.
Canada Laws (PIPEDA): Under the Personal Information Protection and Electronic Documents Act (PIPEDA), personal data must be collected accurately and transparently, and consumers must be informed of the purpose of data usage.
United Kingdom Laws (DPA 2018): Organizations must comply with the Data Protection Act (DPA 2018) in the UK.
Australia Laws (APPs): Under the Australian Privacy Principles (APPs), organizations must adhere to specific privacy principles when collecting and processing data.
Asian Country Laws (e.g., PDPA in Singapore): In compliance with the Personal Data Protection Act (PDPA) in Singapore, organizations must implement methods to maintain privacy and data security for customer personal data.

DD-3-1- If personal data is used for training AI models or other analytical purposes, organizations shall use anonymized or pseudonymized data.

DD-3-2- For any transfer of data to countries outside the region where data protection laws are valid, organizations shall use valid transfer mechanisms, such as Standard Contractual Clauses (SCCs) or similar Privacy Shield agreements.

DD-3-3- At least once a year, organizations shall conduct Privacy Impact Assessments (PIAs) to ensure compliance with data protection laws.

DD-4- Accountability: In case of errors or wrong decisions made by the AI system (such as an incorrect response from a chatbot), a human representative must automatically and quickly intervene and take responsibility for responding to the customer.

DD-5- Inclusion and Equality: AI systems shall be designed to prevent biased data and shall not discriminate against race, gender, religion, or any other characteristic.

EE Specific Requirements:

EE-1- Design of AI Systems: When using chatbots or responsive bots, the maximum customer wait time for an initial response should be one minute and thirty seconds. If the customer's request is complex, the bot must automatically transfer the customer to a human representative after a maximum of 30 seconds (the total wait time should not exceed two minutes).

EE-2- Response Time Across Channels: When responding to phone calls using AI bots, the maximum wait time for the customer should be 2.5 minutes. If the customer cannot speak to a human representative after this time, the call should be disconnected, and an automatic email should be sent for follow-up.

EE-3- Data Analysis: AI systems must have the ability to analyze customer data in real time. For example, chatbots should be capable of detecting and analyzing customer emotions and providing appropriate responses based on those emotions (e.g., happiness, sadness).

EE-4- Compliance with Privacy Laws in AI Processes: All AI models used for customer interactions must follow privacy principles. These models must use customer information minimally and ensure transparency in how data is processed.

Evaluation and Implementation Methods:

EE-5- Model Testing and Validation: Before deploying AI models in CRM systems, A/B testing (testing different variables) must be conducted to evaluate model performance. At least 5,000 interactions must be tested to ensure valid conclusions.

EE-6- Customer Satisfaction Evaluation: At least 90% of customers should be satisfied with their interactions with AI chatbots. This evaluation must be gathered through automated surveys after interactions with the bots.

EE-7-Employee Training: Employees must be trained at least twice a year on how to use AI systems and manage complex customer interactions.

Ethical and Social Issues:

EE-8- Right to Data Correction: Customers must be able to clearly and simply request data correction, deletion, or access through any communication channel (website, app, phone call). The response time for these requests should be a maximum of five business days.

EE-9- Social Impact: Every AI system must prevent potential discrimination. For example, Natural Language Processing (NLP) algorithms should not target customers based on gender or ethnicity due to systemic biases.

Monitoring and Reporting:

EE-10- Reporting and Monitoring: There must be a monitoring system in place that continuously tracks the behavior of AI models. This system should generate monthly reports on system performance and customer satisfaction.

EE-11- Compliance Review: A comprehensive review shall be conducted every six months to assess compliance with this standard, and necessary corrections shall be made if needed.

EE-12- Data Protection Reporting: Organizations shall periodically (at least once a year) provide a transparent report on their compliance with data protection laws across all CRM systems and processes. These reports should include details on compliance with privacy laws of different countries, security breach incidents, and corrective actions taken.

FF Other Requirements:

FF-1-AI in Email Management: AI must be able to accurately segment users based on behaviors, interactions, and demographic information with at least 95% accuracy. AI shall analyze previous email interactions and predict the likelihood of interaction with at least 80% accuracy.

FF-2-Response Time Prediction: AI shall predict the recipient's likely response time with at least 85% accuracy, taking past response trends into account.

FF-3-Subject Line Optimization: AI must suggest at least 5 optimized versions of the subject line that increase the open rate by 10% or more.

FF-4-Automated Voice Messages: Ability to automatically generate personalized voice messages for each potential customer with 90% accuracy in tone and content suitability.

FF-5-Voice Message Delivery Rate: At least 95% of automatically generated voice messages shall be successfully delivered to customers' voicemail.

FF-6-Voice Message Listening Rate: The listening rate should be measured for at least 40% of the total voice messages sent.

FF-7- Internal Dialer: The CRM system shall be able to integrate with existing phone systems so that calls are made directly from the CRM interface with at least 99% uptime.

FF-8- Click-to-Call Feature: At least 95% of click-to-call actions shall initiate calls without error.

FF-9- Call Reports: 100% of calls made or received through the CRM shall be accurately logged, including time, duration, and outcome of the call.

FF-10- Search Performance: Reports shall be searchable by date, duration, and call with a response time of less than 2 seconds.

FF-11- Report Retention: Reports shall be retained for at least 12 months or be adjustable based on business needs.

FF-12-Call Window: The call window shall appear within a maximum of 3 seconds after receiving an inbound call or making an outbound call.

FF-13- Window Display Information: Windows shall display essential information such as the caller's name, call history, and notes with 99% accuracy.

FF-14-Call Recording: All calls shall recorded and available for playback within 1 minute after the call ends.

FF-15- Recording Quality: The audio quality of recordings shall be clear, ensuring at least 98% intelligibility for all parties involved in the call.

FF-16- Recording Storage: Call recordings shall be securely stored for at least 12 months, with an option for archiving or manual deletion.

FF-17-Call Reminder: Call reminders shall start 5 minutes before the scheduled call time with at least 99% accuracy.

FF-18-Reminder Delivery: At least 95% of users shall receive reminders through their preferred channel (email, SMS, or app notification) and be able to customize reminder times with 90% accuracy.

FF-19-Call Scheduling: The call scheduling interface shall allow users to schedule calls with at least 90% accuracy for time zone matching and availability.

FF-20-Time Zone Detection: The CRM system shall automatically detect the customer's time zone with 99% accuracy and adjust the scheduled call accordingly.

FF-21-Scheduling Conflicts: The system shall identify and flag scheduling conflicts if a user attempts to schedule a call at an unauthorized time, with a success rate of at least 98%.

FF-22-Call Tagging: Users shall be able to tag calls with at least 10 predefined tags for categorization (e.g., needs follow-up, hot lead, etc.) and tags shall be applied automatically based on AI analysis or manually with a success rate of 99%.

FF-23-Predefined Responses: At least 10 predefined response templates should be available in each category (e.g., follow-up, request, thank you), with customer satisfaction of at least 80% based on feedback and users shall be able to customize predefined responses with at least 10 fields for personalization (e.g., name, company name).

FF-24-Direct Email Communication: Emails shall be sent from the CRM at the scheduled time with a 99% success rate and delivery confirmation reports shall be generated instantly for 100% of sent emails.

FF-25-Email Integration with CRM Records: Sent or received emails shall automatically link to the appropriate CRM record (contact, deal, etc.) with 99% accuracy and email activities shall be tracked with 100% accuracy and displayed under the corresponding CRM record.

FF-26-Email Client Integration: The CRM system shall seamlessly integrate with at least 5 major email clients (Gmail, Outlook, etc.) and emails, calendars, and contacts shall sync between the CRM and email clients with at least 99% accuracy.

FF-27-Email Scheduling: The system must allow users to schedule emails for future sending with at least a 99% success rate and email scheduling must consider the recipients' time zone with 100% accuracy for timely delivery.

FF-28-Email Status: The CRM system shall track email status with metrics such as open rate, click-through rate, bounce, and delivery success (98% accuracy) and uers shall receive real-time updates on the status of each sent email, including delivery and engagement information.

FF-29-Email Templates: At least 20 pre-built email templates shall be available for various scenarios (sales, follow-up, support, etc.) and templates shall allow for the addition of at least 10 fields for personalization (e.g., recipient name, company name, etc.) and users should be able to edit templates or create custom ones from scratch.

FF-30-Mass Emails: The system shall be able to send at least 10,000 emails in one batch without a decrease in performance and mass emails shall have a delivery rate of at least 95%.

FF-31-Unsubscribe Management: The system should automatically handle unsubscribe requests in full compliance with regulations.

FF-32-SMS Analytics: The system shall provide performance metrics for SMS campaigns, such as delivery rate, open rate, and response rate, with at least 95% accuracy and interaction metrics for each SMS campaign shall be tracked, and automatic reports on interactions and unsubscribe actions shall be provided.

FF-33-SMS Interaction: At least 30% of SMS recipients should respond, based on historical benchmarks. and the system should allow for personalized content insertion in SMS (e.g., recipient's name) with 100% accuracy.

FF-34-SMS Scheduling: Users shall be able to schedule SMS campaigns for sending at a specific time or based on time zones, with at least 99% success rate.

FF-35-Time Zone Awareness: SMS scheduling shall automatically adjust for customers' time zones with 99% accuracy.

FF-36-SMS Templates: At least 10 pre-built SMS templates should be available for different scenarios (advertisements, reminders, etc.) and users should be able to customize templates and save them for future use.

GG Change managment & Continual Improvement:

GG-1-Change Evaluation and Management: Organizations shall implement change management processes for AI systems in CRM and any changes to AI algorithms or technologies shall be thoroughly evaluated and tested before implementation and any changes in AI systems that affect performance or customer experience shall be communicated to customers within 5 business days.

GG-2-Continuous Improvement: The organization shall estabilish a continuous improvement process for AI systems, including periodic performance evaluations, customer feedback collection, and updating algorithms based on new data and AI algorithms shall be updated periodically to ensure optimal performance and adaptability to new challenges.

HH Training and awareness:

HH-1-Customer Training: Customers shall be made aware of how to use and interact with AI systems in CRM. This training shall be provided through websites, apps, and email notifications and customers shall receive sufficient training on how to manage their privacy, including how to access personal data and adjust privacy settings.

HH-2-Employee Training: Employees shall undergo at least one training session annually to improve their skills in using AI and related technologies (such as NLP, machine learning) and be trained on how to manage requests and complex interactions that cannot be processed by AI, ensuring they can effectively respond to customers.

II Validation and Certification:

II-1-Standards Validation: The organizations shall estabilish and implement procedures for various validation methods (e.g., performance tests, internal evaluations) to ensure AI systems comply with this global standard and the organizations shall ensure their CRM systems fully comply with the following two international standards:

ISO 10002:2018 - Customer satisfaction
ISO/IEC 27001:2022 - Information security management systems

II-2-Certification: Only certifying bodies accredited by the relevant accreditation body (a formal member of the International Accreditation Forum (IAF)), which have signed a cooperation agreement with TTAIN (Top Ten Award International Network Inc.), and are listed on (www.TopTenAward.Net), are authorized to carry out audits and issue certificates for this global standard.

JJ Stakeholder and Engagement:

JJ-1-Engagement with Suppliers and Partners: The organizations shall ensure that all their suppliers and business partners who have access to customer data or use AI technologies in CRM processes comply with this Standard.

JJ-2-Reporting to Stakeholders: The organization shall provide annual or periodic reports to stakeholders (such as customers, partners, and legal observers) regarding the use of AI systems and adherence to privacy and data security standards.

KK AI Systems Security:

KK-1-Data and System Security: All AI systems shall use advanced security protocols, such as data encryption, multi-factor authentication, and access control, to prevent unauthorized access to data.

KK-2-Customer sensitive information: All Customer sensitive information shall always be stored in secure environments and comply with global related standards. These data shall be encrypted and protected at all stages of processing.

KK-3-Incident Response Plans: The organization shall have incident response plans for security breaches (e.g., data breaches) and act promptly if an incident occurs. The response time to security incidents shall not exceed 24 hours and any data breach shall be reported to relevant authorities and affected customers within 72 hours.

LL Social Impact Assessment and Review:

LL-1-Social Impact Evaluation: The organization shall conduct a comprehensive evaluation of the social impact of using AI in CRM systems. This evaluation shall include social, economic, and cultural assessments to determine whether AI systems are operating in a discriminatory manner.

LL-2-Social Impact Reporting: The organization shall prepare and publicly release an annual report on the social impact of using AI. These reports should include information on potential discrimination, social issues arising from AI use, and corrective actions taken to address these issues.

MM Documentation and Record keeping:

MM-1-Documentation: The organization shall establish and implement an AI-CRM manual describing all aspects of the application of this standard and all related procedures required for facilitating the implementation of this international standard.

MM-2-Records: The organization shall arrange all necessary actions for keeping records of the implementation of this international standard.

APPENDIX 1
(EXPLANATORY)

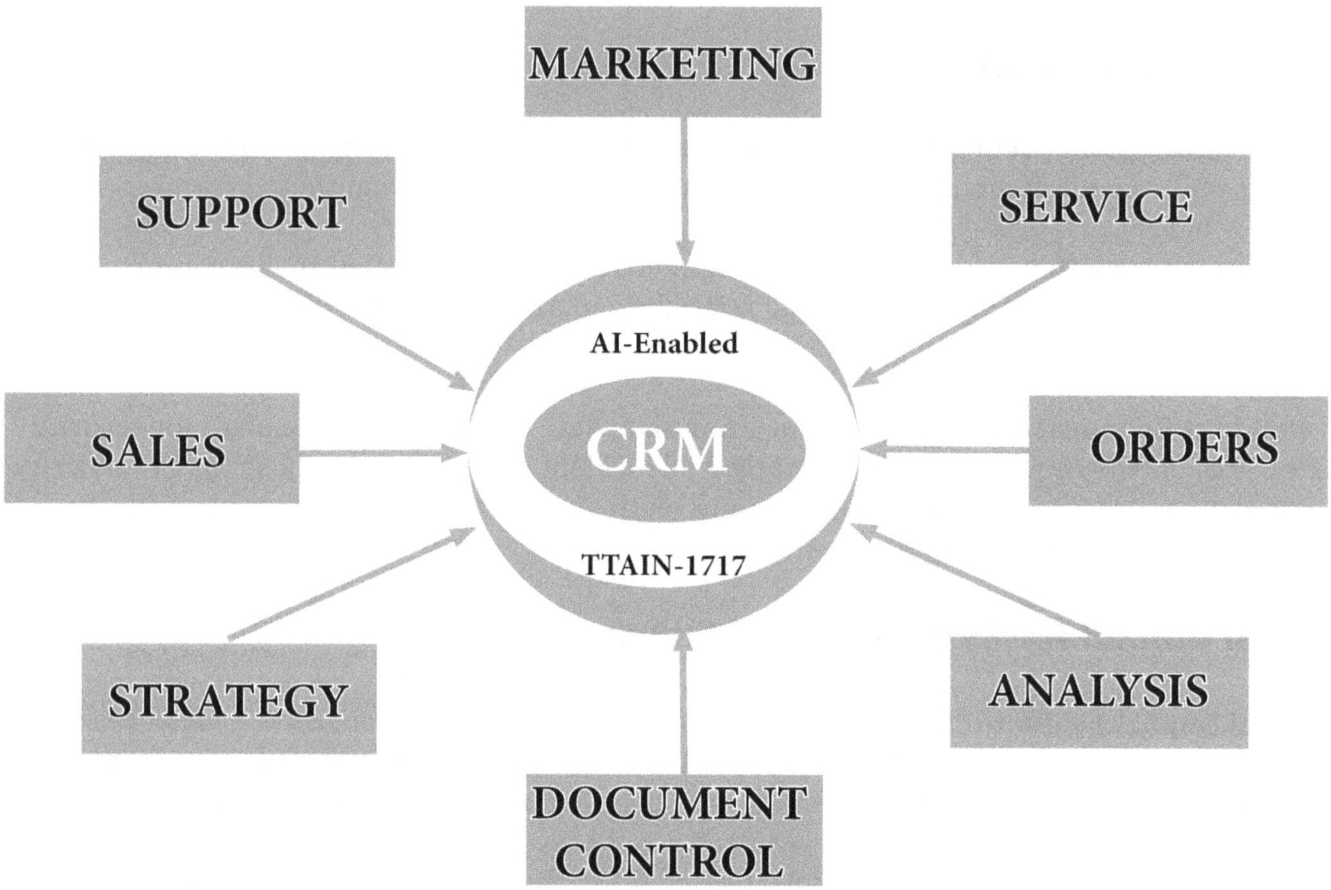

CRM Model Based on: TTAIN-1717

Bibliography:

Anttila, J., & Jussila, K. (2017). ISO 9001:2015- a questionable reform. What should the implementing organisations understand and do? Total Quality Management and Business Excellence, 28(9-10), 1090-1105. https://doi.org/10.1080/14783363.2017.1309119.

Astrini, N. (2018). ISO 9001 and performance: a method review. Total Quality Management & Business Excellence, doi: 10.1080/14783363.2018.1524293.

Abu Ghazaleh, M. and Zabadi, A.M. (2020), "Promoting a revamped CRM through internet of things and big data: an AHP-based evaluation", International Journal of Organizational Analysis, Vol. 28 No. 1, pp. 66-91.

Agostini, L. and Nosella, A. (2019), "Inter-organizational relationships involving SMEs: a bibliographic investigation into the state of the art", Long Range Planning, Vol. 52 No. 1, pp. 1-31.

Anjali Daisy, S. (2020), "Stimulus of chatbot with customer relationship pipeline", Journal of Advanced Research in Dynamical and Control Systems, Vol. 12 No. 5, pp. 885-889, Institute of Advanced Scientific Research, Inc., SASTRA Deemed University, India.

Anshari, M., Alas, Y., Yunus, N., Sabtu, N.I. and Hamid, M.H. (2015), "Social customer relationship management and student empowerment in online learning systems", International Journal of Electronic Customer Relationship Management, Vol. 9 Nos 2/3, pp. 104-121.

Borges, A.F.S., Laurindo, F.J.B., Spínola, M.M., Gonçalves, R.F. and Mattos, C.A. (2020), "The strategic use of artificial intelligence in the digital era: systematic literature review and future research directions", International Journal of Information Management, Vol. 57, p. 102225, Elsevier, No. August.

Boulding, W., Staelin, R., Ehret, M. and Johnston, W.J. (2005), "A customer relationship management roadmap: what is known, potential pitfalls, and where to go", Journal of Marketing, Vol. 69 No. 4, pp. 155-166,No. November 2015.

Boyack, K.W. and Klavans, R. (2010), "Co-citation analysis, bibliographic coupling, and direct citation: which citation approach represents the research front most accurately?", Journal of the American Society for Information Science and Technology, Vol. 61No. 12, pp. 2389-2404.

Bresciani, S., Ciampi, F., Meli, F. and Ferraris, A. (2021), "Using big data for co-innovation processes: mapping the field of data-driven innovation, proposing theoretical developments and providing a research agenda", International Journal of Information Management, Vol. 60, p. 102347, Elsevier Ltd, 20 March.

Brynjolfsson, B.Y.E. and McAfee, A. (2017), "Artificial intelligence for real", Harvard Business Review, Vol. 1, pp. 1-31, July.

BS ISO/IEC 42001:2023, Information technology — Artificial intelligence — Management system

Buckley, R. and Webster, S. (2016), "Fintech in developing countries: charting new customer journeys", Journal of Financial Transformation, Vol. 44, pp. 151-159.

Buttle, F. (2009), Customer Relationship Management: Concepts and Technologies, 4th ed., Routledge, Taylor and Francis Group, Abingdon, Oxon; New York,NY.

Bou-Llusar, J. C., Escrig-Tena, A. B., Roca-Puig, V., & Beltra´n-Martı´n, I. (2005). To what extent do enablers explain results in the EFQM excellence model? International Journal of Quality & Reliability Management, 22(44), 337-353.

Campbell, C., Sands, S., Ferraro, C., Tsao, H.-Y.J. and Mavrommatis, A. (2020), "From data to action: how marketers can leverage AI", Business Horizons, Vol. 63No. 2, pp. 227-243.

Catalan-Matamoros, D. (2012), "An overview to customer relationship management", in Catalan-Matamoros, D. (Eds), Advances in Customer Relationship Management, IntechOpen, London. Chang, J.W., Lee, M.C. and Wang, T.I. (2016), "Integrating a semantic-based retrieval agent into case-based reasoning systems: a case study of an online bookstore", Computers in Industry, Vol. 78, pp. 29-42.

Chang, V. (2018), "A proposed social network analysis platform for big data analytics", Technological Forecasting and Social Change, Vol. 130, pp. 57-68.

Chatzoglou, P., Chatzoudes, D., & Kipraios, N. (2015). The impact of ISO 9000 certification on firms' financial performance. International Journal of Operations and Production Management, 35(1), 145-174.
Chatterjee, S., Ghosh, S.K., Chaudhuri, R. and Nguyen, B. (2019), "Are CRM systems ready for AI integration?: a conceptual framework of organizational readiness for effective AI-CRM integration", The Bottom Line, Vol. 32 No. 2, pp. 144-157.
Chatterjee, S., Ghosh, S.K. and Chaudhuri, R. (2020a), "Knowledge management in improving business process: an interpretative framework for successful implementation of AI–CRM–KM system in organizations", Business Process Management Journal, Vol. 26 No. 6, pp. 1261-1281, doi: 10.1108/BPMJ-05-2019-0183.
Chiang, W.Y. (2019), "Establishing high value markets for data-driven customer relationship management systems: an empirical case study", Kybernetes, Vol. 48 No. 3, pp. 650-662.
Chiarini, A. (2017). Risk-based thinking according to ISO 9001:2015 standard and the risk sources European manufacturing SMEs intend to manage. The TQM Journal, 29(2), 310-323. https://doi.org/10.1108/TQM-04-2016-0038.
De Caigny, A., Coussement, K. and De Bock, K.W. (2020a), "Leveraging fine-grained transaction data for customer life event predictions", Decision Support Systems, Vol. 130, p. 113232, doi: 10.1016/j.dss.2019.113232.
De Caigny, A., Coussement, K., De Bock, K.W. and Lessmann, S. (2020b), "Incorporating textual information in customer churn prediction models based on a convolutional neural network", International Journal of Forecasting, Vol. 36 No. 4, pp. 1563-1578, doi: 10.1016/j.ijforecast.2019.03.029.
Del Vecchio, P., Mele, G., Passiante, G., Vrontis, D. and Fanuli, C. (2020), "Detecting customers knowledge from social media big data: toward an integrated methodological framework based on netnography and business analytics", Journal of Knowledge Management, Vol. 24 No. 4, pp. 799-821.
Deshpande, A. and Kumar, M. (2018), "Artificial intelligence for big data", Journal of Chemical Information and Modeling, Vol. 53No. 9, pp. 1689-1699.
Donthu, N., Kumar, S., Mukherjee, D., Pandey, N. and Lim, W.M. (2021), "How to conduct a bibliometric analysis: an overview and guidelines", Journal of Business Research, Vol. 133, pp. 285-296,No. March.
El Fazziki, A., Ennaji, F.Z., Sadiq, A., Benslimane, D. and Sadgal, M. (2017), "A multi-agent based social crm framework for extracting and analysing opinions", Journal of Engineering Science and Technology, Vol. 12 No. 8, pp. 2154-2174.
Grover, V., Chiang, R.H.L., Liang, T.-P. and Zhang, D. (2018), "Creating strategic business value from big data analytics: a research framework", Journal of Management Information Systems, Vol. 35 No. 2, pp. 388-423.
Hallikainen, H., Savimäki, E. and Laukkanen, T. (2020), "Fostering B2B sales with customer big data analytics", Industrial MarketingManagement, Vol. 86, pp. 90-98.
Domingues, J. P. T., Sampaio, P., & Arezes, P. M. (2016). Integrated management systems assessment: a maturity model proposal. Journal of Cleaner Production, 124, 164-174, doi: 10.1016/j.jclepro.2016.02.103
Hopkinson, P.J. and Singhal, A. (2018), "Exploring the use of AI to manage customers' relationships", in 51st Academy of Marketing Conference, University of Stirling, United Kingdom, pp. 1-7.
Iansiti, M. and Lakhani, K.R. (2020), Competing in the Age of AI: Strategy and Leadership When Algorithms and Networks Run the World,Harvard Business Review Press, Boston.
ISO 10002:2018, Quality management — Customer satisfaction — Guidelines for complaints handling in organizations
ISO/IEC 27001:2022, Information security, cybersecurity and privacy protection — Information security management systems — Requirements
Kahneman, D., Tversky, A. and Tversky, A. (1979), "Prospect theory: an analysis of decision under risk", Econometrica, Vol. 47No. 2, pp. 263-292.
Kaplan, A. and Haenlein, M. (2019), "Siri, Siri, in my hand: who's the fairest in the land? On the interpretations, illustrations, and implications of artificial intelligence", Business Horizons, Vol. 62 No. 1, pp. 15-25, "Kelley School of Business, Indiana University".

Khan, G.F. and Wood, J. (2015), "Information technology management domain: emerging themes and keyword analysis", Scientometrics, Vol. 105 No. 2, pp. 959-972, Springer Netherlands.

Khodakarami, F. and Chan, Y.E. (2014), "Exploring the role of customer relationship management (CRM) systems in customer knowledge creation", Information & Management, Vol. 51No. 1, pp. 27-42.

Kietzmann, J. and Pitt, L.F. (2020), "Computerized content analysis of online data – opportunities for marketing scholars and practitioners", European Journal of Marketing, Vol. 54 No. 3, pp. 473-477.

Lokuge, S., Sedera, D., Kumar, S., Ariyachandra, T. and Ravi, V. (2020), "The next wave of CRM innovation: implications for research, teaching, and practice", Communications of the Association for Information Systems, Vol. 46, pp. 560-583.

Loureiro, S.M.C., Guerreiro, J. and Tussyadiah, I. (2021), "Artificial intelligence in business: state of the art and future research agenda", Journal of Business Research, Vol. 129, pp. 911-926, doi: 10.1016/j.jbusres.2020.11.001,No. May.

McCain, K.W. (1990), "Mapping authors in intellectual space: a technical overview", Journal of the American Society for Information Science, Vol. 41 No. 6, p. 433.

McColl-Kennedy, J.R., Zaki, M., Lemon, K.N., Urmetzer, F. and Neely, A. (2019), "Gaining customer experience insights that matter", Journal of Service Research, Vol. 22 No. 1, pp. 8-26.

Maklan, S., Peppard, J. and Klaus, P. (2015), "Show me the money improving our understanding of how organizations generate return from technology-led marketing change", European Journal of Marketing, Vol. 49Nos 3/4, pp. 561-595.

Manna, R. and Nath, R. (2021), "The problem of moral agency in artificial intelligence", paper presented at IEEE Conference on Norbert Wiener in the 21st Century: BeingHuman in aGlobal Village, 22-25 July 2021, CEG Campus, Anna University Chennai.

Marchiori, D. and Franco, M. (2020), "Knowledge transfer in the context of inter-organizational networks: foundations and intellectual structures", Journal of Innovation & Knowledge, Vol. 5 No. 2, pp. 130-139.

Niknejad, N., Ismail,W., Bahari, M., Hendradi, R. and Salleh, A.Z. (2021), "Mapping the research trends on blockchain technology in food and agriculture industry: a bibliometric analysis", Environmental Technology & Innovation, Vol. 21, p. 101272.

Ojo, A. and Rizun, N. (2019), "Enabling deeper linguisticbased text analytics – construct development for the criticality of negative service experience", IEEE Access, Vol. 7, pp. 169217-169256, doi: 10.1109/ACCESS.2019.2947593.

Payne, A. and Frow, P. (2005), "A strategic framework for customer relationship management", Journal of Marketing, Vol. 69No. 4, pp. 167-176.

Pearson, A. (2019), "Personalisation the artificial intelligence way", Journal of Digital and Social Media Marketing, Vol. 7 No. 3, pp. 245-269.

Trivedi, J. (2019), "Examining the customer experience of using banking chatbots and its impact on brand love: the moderating role of perceived risk", Journal of Internet Commerce, Vol. 18No. 1, pp. 91-111.

Van Eck, N.J. and Waltman, L. (2010), "Software survey: VOSviewer, a computer program for bibliometric mapping", Scientometrics, Vol. 84No. 2, pp. 523-538.

Van Eck, N.J. and Waltman, L. (2020), "Manual for VOSviewer version 1.6.15. Vignesh, R. and Vasantha, S. (2019), "Significant developments of artificial intelligence in Indian ecommerce industry in 2019", International Journal of Scientific and Technology Research, Vol. 8 No. 12, pp. 2746-2748.

Williamson, O.E. (1979), "Transaction-cost economics: the governance of contractual relations", The Journal of Law and Economics, Vol. 22No. 2, pp. 233-261.

Wilson-Nash, C., Goode, A. and Currie, A. (2020), "Introducing the socialbot: a novel touchpoint along the young adult customer journey", European Journal of Marketing, Vol. 54 No. 10, pp. 2621-2643, doi: 10.1108/EJM-07-2019-0555.

Yi, Z. (2018), "The application of clustering in customer management based on big data", IPPTA: Quarterly Journal of Indian Pulp and Paper Technical Association, Vol. 30 No. 8, pp. 718-722, Indian Pulp and Paper Technical Association, Sichuan University of Media and Communications, Xinxiang, Henan, 611745, China.

Zaki, M. (2019), "Digital transformation: harnessing digital technologies for the next generation of services", Journal of

Services Marketing, Vol. 33 No. 4, pp. 429-435. Zerbino, P., Aloini, D., Dulmin, R. and Mininno, V. (2018), "Big data-enabled customer relationship management: a holistic approach", Information Processing & Management, Vol. 54No. 5, pp. 818-846.

www.ingramcontent.com/pod-product-compliance
Lightning Source LLC
LaVergne TN
LVHW060046210926
848481LV00013B/3965